Warsaw

and surroundings

TEXT: RAFAŁ JABŁOŃSKI
PHOTOGRAPHY: STANISŁAWA, JOLANTA
AND RAFAŁ JABŁOŃSKI

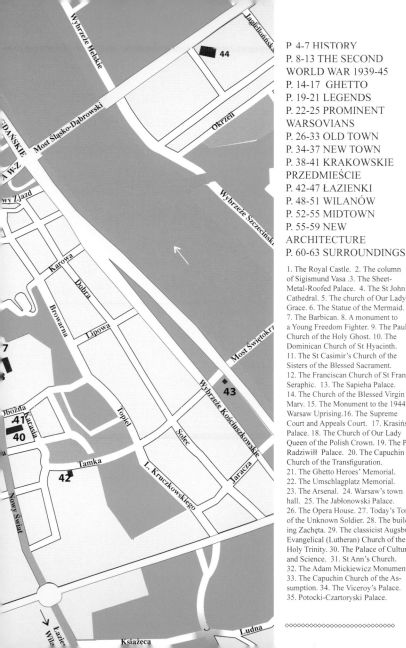

1. The Royal Castle. 2. The column of Sigismund Vasa .3. The Sheet-Metal-Roofed Palace. 4. The St John's Cathedral. 5. The church of Our Lady of Grace. 6. The Statue of the Mermaid. 7. The Barbican. 8. A monument to a Young Freedom Fighter. 9. The Pauline Church of the Holy Ghost. 10. The Dominican Church of St Hyacinth. 11. The St Casimir's Church of the Sisters of the Blessed Sacrament. 12. The Franciscan Church of St Francis Seraphic. 13. The Sapieha Palace. 14. The Church of the Blessed Virgin Mary. 15. The Monument to the 1944 Warsaw Uprising.16. The Supreme Court and Appeals Court. 17. Krasiński Palace. 18. The Church of Our Lady Queen of the Polish Crown. 19. The Pac-Radziwiłł Palace. 20. The Capuchin Church of the Transfiguration. 21. The Ghetto Heroes' Memorial. 22. The Umschlagplatz Memorial. 23. The Arsenal. 24. Warsaw's town hall. 25. The Jabłonowski Palace. 26. The Opera House. 27. Today's Tomb of the Unknown Soldier. 28. The building Zachęta. 29. The classicist Augsburg Evangelical (Lutheran) Church of the Holy Trinity. 30. The Palace of Culture and Science. 31. St Ann's Church. 32. The Adam Mickiewicz Monument. 33. The Capuchin Church of the Assumption. 34. The Viceroy's Palace. 35. Potocki-Czartoryski Palace.

Introduction

Warsaw, Europe's youngest capital, is a city with a long history. Already in the 10th century, in the region of today's right-bank Bródno district there existed a fortified-town complex. In the centuries that followed, the settlements of Kamion, Targowe Wielkie and Solec developed. The latter was protected by a fortified castle town known as Jazdów and situated on the site of today's Botanical Gardens. Destroyed by invading Lithuanian Jadvingian barbarians, it was rebuilt at a different, more defensible site. Bolesław II, the Duke of Masovia, probably chose the site because of its tall escarpment and superior water supply from the Rivers Drna and Bełczącej (now the East-West Thorough-

Warsaw Panorama seen from the Vistula, wood-c of AD 1589".

fare). The town was named Warszawa (Warszowa) from the name Warsz that was frequently encountered in the Rawicz-Niedźwiadek clan which owned the nearby village of Solec. In time, a powerful castle was erected at that site, and the town began developing to the south of it and was walled in. The then popular chessboard layout with a central marketplace was used. St John's Church was built, a wójt (local administrator) was chosen and a Town Council deliberated in the town

Sejm of Poland in the end of the 17th century, a copperplate of Charles de La Haye.

...he "Constitution of the General Assembly

district's commercial character was attested to by its numerous granaries, storehouses and workshops. Defensive walls were not erected, however.

Warsaw's further development was affected by the rise of jurisdictions. Those were private aristocrat-owned towns not subject to the municipal authorities. They had their own administration, and some of them also had their own marketplace and town hall. They survived till the end of the 18th century.

Warsaw's central location gained in importance as the borders of the Royal Republic and subsequently - after the Polish-Lithuanian union - the Commonwealth of Two Nations expanded. It was there that the important transport routes converged and, from 1569, national General Crown Assemblies took place. Representatives of the aristocracy and gentry would come to

hall erected in the late 14th and early 15th centuries.

Duke Janusz I the Elder resolved to make Warsaw the capital of the Duchy of Masovia. Important ducal assemblies began taking place and the earthly remains of successive Masovian rulers were laid to rest in St John's Church. At the start of the 14th century, beyond the New Town Gate. a new commercial settlement known as New Town began emerging. A marketplace with a town hall was also laid out, and the

View of Warsaw, 18th-century engraving by Bernardo Bellotto-Canaletto.

such assemblies from every corner of the land. From 1573, elections of Polish kings were held in the fields of Wola. The third successive electoral assembly elected Swedish-born Zygmunt III Vasa as king. Following the fire at Kraków's Wawel Castle in 1596, the king decided to move the capital from Kraków to Warsaw. Apart from considerations of state, the king's decision was influenced by his nostalgia for his homeland, so remote from Kraków. Warsaw

View of the Old Town Marketplace in 1900.

View of Warsaw according to a copper engraving in a 1662 book by S. Stawicki.

became the country's political and economic centre. Aristocrats, noblemen, artists and traders would gather at the court for which the castle was renovated. As more and more people flocked to the town, it began to grow and make room for new palaces and dwelling-houses.

During the reigns of the Saxon Dynasty (King August II and III) a short-lived construction boom occurred. Work was conducted at the Royal Castle where new chambers were created, headed by the impressive Deputies' Chamber. It was there on 3 May 1791 that Europe's first democratic constitutions was adopted.

Warsaw entered a period of dynamic development during the reign of Poland's last king, Stanisław August Poniatowski. The best architects renovated the Royal Castle, and the old

Lubomirski bathhouses was transformed into the king's summer residence.

The period of Poland's partitions, which lasted with interruptions for 120 years, reduced Warsaw to the rank of a provincial town. Armed uprisings such as the Kościuszko Insurrection, the November Insurrection and January Insurrection only increased the reprisals on the part of the occupying powers.

Total renewal came only when Poland regained its independence in 1918. New districts -Żoliborz, Bielany and Saska Kępa - were developed. An airport was built in Okęcie.

The year 1939 augured Warsaw's further destruction. Already on 1 September, its inhabitants were subjected to a German bombardment in which the Royal Castle caught fire. Warsaw's total destruction occurred in 1944. After the 63-day Warsaw Uprising, the Germans systematically looted and set fire to the city.

Immediately after the war ended, the people of Warsaw set about raising their city from the rubble. Old Town as well as most palaces and historic dwelling-houses were rebuilt.

But the true development of Warsaw began only after 1989 in the Third Republic. The restoration of democracy and a market economy enabled its inhabitants to make up for the time

Warsaw Uprising. An insurgent in battle.

they lost during the communist period. The encroachment of modernity can be seen at every turn.

Old Town Square in 1945.

Bombardment of Warsaw, September 1939.

On 1st September 1939, German forces launched an assault against Poland, attacking it from three sides. Germany's overwhelming odds soon led to the collapse of Poland's armed resistance. Already on 8th September, Warsaw was attacked by the first German trios if General Reinhardt's Fourth Armoured Division, and by 13th-15th September the entire city was surrounded. Warsaw's mayor and civil-defence commissioner Stefan Starzyński refused to join the evacuation of the Polish government and took command of the city's defence efforts. He became famous for his fiery radio addresses which inspired the nation's spirit of resistance.

Following the Soviet Union's aggression against Poland on 17th September 1939, the Nazis began escalating their war operations. The German-Soviet agreement linked the partition of Poland with the capitulation of its capital. On 17th September, the Germans bombed Warsaw's Royal Castle, and on the 25th carried out carpet bombings which destroyed 12 percent of the city's buildings. 10,000 Warsaw residents perished and 35,000 were wounded as a result.

Warsaw finally capitulated on 28th September, and two days later the first German troops marched into the city. Some 120,000 Polish soldiers were captured. The Nazi occupation, which would be marked by acts of terror, had begun. On 26th October, the Germans created on Polish soil an administrative entity known as the General Government with

Royal Castle in 1939.

its capital in Kraków. In reprisal for putting up resistance, Warsaw was to remain in ruins, and the Germans planned to demolish the Royal Castle which had already been damaged by aerial bombings. In accordance with the guidelines Hitler gave General Governor Hans Frank on 4th November, Warsaw was to be reduced to the status of a provincial town. A curfew was imposed, arrests (especially of the Warsaw intelligentsia), executions and deportations to concentration camps got under way. The place political prisoners were detained was Pawiak Prison, from which they were sent to such execution sites in the Warsaw areas as Palmiry. The Gestapo prison at Aleja Szucha was where people caught in street round-ups were tortured.

The defenders of Warsaw in September 1939.

Nevertheless, the spirit of resistance among the people of Warsaw did not disappear. Already on 27th September 1939 an underground organisation called Polish Victory Service emerged. In November it was renamed the Armed Combat Union under the command of Colonel Stefan Rowecki, cryptonym Grot. By orders of General Władysław Sikorski in 1942, it was transformed into the Home Army.

The Polish Scouting Union, known by the cryptonym Grey Ranks, was also involved in the underground movement. Warsaw may have ceased being the capital of the Polish state, but it became the capital of the Polish Underground State. That clandestine entity issues newspapers, rescued architectural relics, conducted underground educational and cultural activities and, above all, engaged in numerous combat actions and acts of sabotage. Up until 1942, the authorities of the Armed Combat Union promoted passive resistance to the occupation forces to avoid German reprisals against the citizenry. Only limited sabotage and organisational activities were conducted, including the acquisition of weapons, intelligence and counter-intelligence efforts as well as combating informers.

In 1942, the political situation changed. The Germans began suffering defeats on all fronts, and terror against the townspeople of Warsaw was stepped up. As a result, the resistance movement modi-

The young insurgents.

fied its tactics to include more intensive forms of struggle against the occupation forces. In 1943, a structure known as Kedyw was formed within the Home Army to organised armed struggle. The number of armed actions conducted by various units increased and included attacks on Nazi functionaries. One of the most spectacular was the 1944 assassination of General-Major Franz Kutschera, the Warsaw SS and police commander. There were also numerous actions to spring prisoners. The best known occurred outside the arsenal in 1944, when Jan Bytnar was freed from Gestapo detention.

As Soviet forces neared Warsaw, there were fears that Polish territory could become subordinated to the USSR, the more so that on 21st July 1944 a Polish Committee of National Liberation controlled by our eastern neighbour had been set up. The Home Army drew up a plan code-named Storm involving an attack on the Germans' rear lines so as to be able to present themselves to the Soviet authorities as the authentic representatives of the Polish nation. On 26th July, the London-based Polish Government-in-Exile authorised Home Army Commander General Bor-Komorowski to launch an insurrection in

Warsaw When Soviet troops appeared on the outskirts of Warsaw, on 31st July the decision was taken begin the armed struggle the following day at 5 PM, code-named W hour.

In the first days of the struggle, the insurrectionists numbered 50,000. They were armed with only 1,000 rifles, 300 automatic weapons, several grenade launchers, mortars and armour-piercing weapons, 40,000 hand grenades and 12,000 Molotov cocktails. Initially, the German side numbered some 15,000 troops, reinforced on 3rd-4th September by SS and police units. They were superbly armed with heavy and automatic weapons as well as tanks and armoured vehicles. The German forces were con-

Warsaw insurgents emerging from the sewers, 1944.

Insurgents "Rybak" and "Kajtek".

centrated in specially prepared fortified bunkers surrounded by barbed wire. The outbreak of the Warsaw Uprising took Hitler by surprise and infuriated him. In agreement with Himmler, he issued order No. 1 which commanded: "Every inhabitant should be killed. Warsaw is to be levelled to the ground so as to set an intimidating example for all of Europe. And no prisoners of war are to be taken".

At the same time, Stalin, who regarded Warsaw and Fortress Modlin as strategic points, on 5th august had issued an order to halt all military operations on the Warsaw front and intensify efforts in other areas. The Soviets even stopped short of capturing Okęcie Airport, from which air raids against Warsaw had been launched – a move that astonished the Germans themselves. Supply flights by the Western allies were obstructed, and those outlying Home Army units capable of reinforcing the insurgents were particularly combated. Plans to encircle Warsaw were drawn up, but their implementation was postponed for five weeks. By the same token, Stalin had sealed Warsaw's fate.

The Germans stationed in Warsaw had obtained information on the outbreak of the uprising. As a result, the initial Polish assault was not as successful as expected. After regrouping, on 5th August the Germans launched a counterattack which forced Polish units to defend isolated districts of the city. They built barricades in the streets and fought over

Bombardment of Warsaw, September 1939.

every building and inch of land. The civilian population, including children, took part in the struggle. Unable to quash the rebellion in a single blow, the occupation forces decided on scorched-land tactics. They deployed flame-throwers, artillery and remote-controlled mines of the Goliath and Typhoon type, filled with powerful explosives.

RAF planes, some piloted by Poles, began supply drops to the insurgents on 4th August. Unfortunately, due to heavy plane losses and the limited insurgent-controlled drop areas, of the 230 tonnes of supplies dropped over Warsaw only less than 50 tonnes reached the Polish freedom-fighters.

On 13th-15th September, the Soviet offensive dislodge the Germans from right-bank Warsaw, and on 16th-22nd September, the 1st Army of the Soviet-backed Polish Armed Forces crossed the Vistula, establishing beach-heads at Czerniaków, Powiśle and Żoliborz. But without the support of the main Soviet forces, the landing proved unsuccessful. The struggle in left-bank Warsaw continued, but the resistance of the insurgents gradually waned, and the Germans succeeded in recapturing one district after another. After the fall of Old Town, the insurrectionists made their way through the sewers to the City Centre, where they continued thee struggle. Żoliborz held out the longest until 30th September.

The act of capitulation was signed on the night of 2nd-3rd October in Ożarów.

Old Town Square (Kołłqtaj side) in 1945.

The insurgent losses were staggering. Of the 50,000 insurrectionists, some 10,000 had been killed, and 25,000 had been wounded. Civilian losses came to 150,000. About 25 percent of the city's buildings had been reduced to rubble, and all its monuments, public buildings and bridges lay in ruins. Following the capitulation, the Germans began demolishing the city with explosives and flame/throwers. By January 1945, 70 percent of the city lay in ruins

The balance-sheet of the Warsaw Uprising is an ambiguous one. It was unique in occupied Europe, since no other city had managed to hold out so long and involve so many residents in the struggle. It was also a desperate attempt to maintain the country's independence against Stalin's imposition of communist rule as symbolised by the Polish Committee of National Liberation. But betrayed by its allies in September 1939 and in Teheran in 1943, Poland had no chance of achieving that goal. The spheres of influence had been delimited. All the Polish nation retained was its honour and the message going out into the world: this is how the Polish nation fights for freedom.

Jews being led out of the ghetto.

From the first days of the German occupation in Warsaw, people of Jewish ancestry were subjected to different treatment than the rest of the local community. The occupiers regarded as Jews all those who had at least three grandparents belonging to a Jewish religious congregation. As a result, many assimilated individuals who regarded themselves as Poles or even espoused the Christian faith suffered persecution. From 1st December 1939, Jews were obliged to wear arm-bands displaying the Star of David which facilitated German harassment and reprisals such as being robbed, beaten are having beards shorn off. Their bank accounts were blocked, Jewish book shops and schools were closed, Jews were banned from travelling by train and a were restricted to special section in Warsaw's trams. Forced labour was imposed for which the only payment was a modest meal. In 1940, anti-Jewish actions financed by the Germans and used for propaganda purposes began. Nevertheless, many people of Jewish ancestry migrated to Warsaw from front areas incorporated into the Reich and from outlying areas. Round the start of 1940, preparations to create a separate district for Jews got under way. A directive of 2nd October 1940, signed by Governor Fischer, ordered all Jews to be moved into the ghetto. On 16th November, the Jewish Residential District was surrounded by a three-metre-tall wall topped with barbed wire. About 450,000 Jews were herded into an area of some 307 hectares. It consisted of two parts: the big ghetto and the little ghetto, linked by a wooden foot bridge over Chłodna street which was part of the Arian district. Administrative duties were entrusted to the Jewish Council or Judenrat and the Jewish Order-Keeping Service, a hated police formation which took orders from the German authorities. The living and sanitary conditions in the ghetto were deplorable. With 146,000 inhabitants per square kilometre, things were congested and there were eight to ten people per room. Refuse was not removed, causing the spread of various

Warsaw Ghetto. The bodies of murdered Jews, April 1943.

diseases. Often corpses were not buried for several days. The property of ghetto inhabitants had been confiscated and they had no source of income. Food rations were often less than 200 calories a day, so people's main preoccupation was finding something to eat. There was large-scale smuggling by crimina gangs. Help came from beyond the ghetto, smuggled in through tunnels, openings in the wall or by bribed German policemen. Especially useful in such proceedings were Jewish children who could easily come and go through openings and sewers. Children were also smuggled out of the ghetto, and in that wave their lives were saved. Mortality in the ghetto was extremely high, and by July 1942 some 100,000 people had died. On 22nd July 1944, a cordon of German and Jewish police surrounded the ghetto and announced the compulsory removal of its population "to the east". Everyone was allowed to take along 15 kilograms of luggage, money and valuables.

A daily quota was initially set at 6,000

Arm-band vendor in the ghetto, 1940.

Wall of the Warsaw Ghetto, 1940

people and subsequently increased. The operation was conducted in such a way that one by one buildings or sections of the ghetto were surrounded and all its tenants were thrown out of their flats. Anyone who resisted was killed on the spot. Columns of people were formed and driven to what was known as the Umschlagplatz (reloading point) at Stawki Street, connected by a side track to Gdańsk Railway Station. People were beaten with batons, shoved and herded into cattle wagons headed east. The few that managed to flee from the transport after several days brought the tragic news that the trains were travelling to Treblinka Station not far from the town of Małkinia, where a mass-extermination camp fitted with gas chamber had been set up. The trains retuned to Warsaw empty. In spite of that information, the Jewish population passively went to its death. After the Germans announced that everyone who volunteered would get three kilos of bread and jam for the road and that families would not be separated, crowds

of starving, sick people came forward. The first to be transported were those of no use to the German war machine. Entire shelters, hospitals and children's care institutions were evacuated. It was on 5th August 1942 that Janusz Korczak, the outstanding writer and pedagogue, went to his death at the head of columns of children from his orphanage. In September, Judenrat employees and members of the Jewish police were carted away despite the fact that they had served the Nazis.

The deportation campaign lasted until 21st September 1942 and involved some 310,000 Jews. Following that action, only some 30,000 people holding able-bodied worker's certificates and as many more living there illegally remained in the ghetto. On 16th April, Himmler ordered the liquidation of the entire ghetto. On 18th April, the Germans tried to carry out another evacuation but met with active resistance which by the following day had

Ruins of the Warsaw Ghetto.

Church of Sts. Augustine. The only building not destroyed the Warsaw Ghetto.

escalated into an open revolt. The resistance put up by Jewish units took the Germans completely by surprise. By 2 PM all the German troops were driven out of the ghetto, suffering serious losses. The Germans changed their tactics and decided to demolish and torch the buildings in the ghetto one by one. The glow of fires could be seen over the city. The new method was producing results. On 8th May, the bunker housing the Jewish Combat Organisation's headquarters, commanded by Mordechaj Anielewicz, was discovered. Unable to mount a defence, he committed suicide. On 16th May, German commander Colonel Jürgen

Stroop ordered the Great Synagogue at Tłomackie Street to be blown up, proclaiming that the day the Warsaw Residential District was destroyed. The Warsaw Ghetto was levelled to the ground with the exception of several churches and Pawiak Prison. Most of the ghetto's inhabitants had been killed in the fighting or were taken to Majdanek where they were put to death in gas chambers. Only a small group of fugitives, who had made it over to the Polish side, managed to survive.

WARS AND SAWA

Long, long ago, on the banks of the Vistula stood a tiny hut inhabited by the fisherman Wars and his wife Sawa. One day, the local lord Ziemiomysł was hunting in the vicinity. In pursuit of game, he had wandered away from his party and lost his way in the forest. Evening was already approaching when he reached the banks of the Vistula and spotted the hut of Wars and Sawa. Since wandering in the forest at night was dangerous, the prince knocked on the door and requested shelter. Wars and Sawa lavished their hospitality upon him, fed him and offered him a place to stay – an offer that was gratefully accepted. The next morning, the prince thanked the poor fisherfolk for their help and was said to have told them: "You did not hesitate to receive a stranger under your roof and rescued him from hunger, cold and perhaps even from wild beasts. Therefore these lands will for ever more be known

Wars and Sawa Monument.

as Warszowa, so your kindness shall not be forgotten".

Basilisk.

BASILISK

Long, long ago, in the cellar of a house at Krzywe Koło Street there lived a ferocious monster known as the Basilisk, who had hatched from an egg laid by a seven-year-old cock and bred by a poisonous viper.

He had the head of a cock and the body of a spiny serpent. The dungeon watched over by the Basilisk contained numerous treasures, but no-one could get at them, because the Basilisk could kill just by looking at someone. Whoever he looked at turned to stone.

One day, a brave young cobbler decided to capture the treasure guarded over by the Basilisk. After giving a lot of thought to how he would outfox the monster, he took a mirror from one of the Old Town stalls and took it down to the cellar. When he heard the roar of the approaching, he moved the mirror out in front of it. The Basilisk saw its reflection and turned to stone at the sight of its own image. Thanks to his ruse, the clever young cobbler acquired great wealth.

THE GOLDEN DUCK

Many, many years ago, in the small subterranean lake in the grottos below Ostrogski Palace swam a small duck with golden feathers. It was said to be an enchanted princess who was guarding over immense treasures.

Legends about those treasures abounded amongst the Warsaw townsfolk, but nobody succeeded in capturing them. A poor cobbler decided to search for the treasures, made his way into the grottos and indeed encountered the golden duck The duck proposed a test: the cobbler would get 100 ducats, all of which he must spend before sundown, but only

Golden Duck at Tamka Street fountain..

The Mermaid on the Markiewicz viaduct.

hat. At that moment, everything he had bought suddenly vanished and he found himself dressed in his old, shabby garb. Since he had not kept his end of the bargain, the magic spell burst. The old solider sympathised with him and consoled him by saying the fortune he earned through honest toil would always be his and would be command the gratitude and respect of others.

THE MERMAID

It was ages ago that two mermaid sisters, beautiful women with fish tails who had lived in the depths of the sea, swam into the Baltic from the Atlantic. One of

on himself, as he may not share it with others. If he succeeded, he would get the entire treasure. But if he failed, everything he bought would disappear and eh would never again find his way into the grotto. The cobbler agreed to those terms. At sunrise he set out to go shopping. All day he kept spending the money he had got from the duck. He had new, elegant outfits custom-tailored, bought a gold carriage, ate, drank and spent money left and right. Before nightfall he still had one ducat left.

Returning to the palace, he saw an old solider, a war veteran begging for a crust of bread. Seeing him, the cobbler dropped his last coin into the beggar's

Mermaid at the Wybrzeże Kościuszkowskie rivers

them took a fancy to the cliffs of the Straits of Denmark, and to this day she may be seen sitting on a rock at the entrance to the Port of Copenhagen.

The other mermaid swam to Gdańsk, a great Baltic port, and then travelled down the Vistula. According to legend, she left the water at the foot of today's New Town, more or less where her statue now stands, and rested on the sandy riverbank. Since the area appealed to her, she decided to stay. Local fishermen soon noticed that someone was stirring up the waters of the Vistula, knotting up their nets and releasing the fish they had caught. But since they were charmed by the mermaid's singing, they did nothing about it

A wealthy merchant once saw the mermaid and her splendid singing. He calculated how much he would earn if he captured the mermaid and began showing her at fairs. He deceptively captured the mermaid and locked her in a wooden shed with no access to water. The mermaid's plaintive cries were heard by a young farmhand, a fisherman's son and together with a group of friends freed her under the cover of night. In gratitude, the mermaid told the townsfolk they could always count on her in times of need. That is why the Warsaw mermaid is armed with a sword and shield – to defend the town.

The Syrena (Mermaid) factory from 1957 to 1983.

FRYDERYK CHOPIN (1810-49)

Fryderyk Chopin (1810-49) - the outstanding, world-renowned composer and pianist was born at Żelazowa Wola near Łowicz to the family of Mikołaj Chopin, a Frenchman from Lorraine, and Polish noblewoman, Justyna Krzyżanowska. Chopin's father was employed at Żelazowa Wola as the home tutor of Count Fryderyk Skarbek, the proprietor of the local estate. The Chopin family lived in one of the annexes of the no longer existing Żelazowa Wola manor house. Both of Fryderyk's parents were musically inclined: his father played the violin and flute and his mother - the piano.

Already in autumn 1810, the Chopin family moved to Warsaw. There Fryderyk took piano lessons, at first with his mother and later with Wojciech Żywny, a Czech.

Fryderyk Chopin by Eugène Delacroix

There Chopin first tried his hand at composition at the age of seven, and two polonaises-in G Minor and B Major-were the result. At the age of eight, Fryderyk gave his first public performance to the delight of Warsaw's salons, where he became a sought-after attraction. When he turned 15, his first two mazurkas-in G Major and Rondo in C Minor-appeared in print. In 1826-29, Chopin developed his talent at the Main School of Music under the tutelage of Józef Elsner. Exempted from having to take further piano lessons owing to this unique playing style, he studied composition and harmony. Following a short sojourn in Vienna, he travelled to Paris, where he settled permanently. Bid farewell by his friends at the outskirts of Warsaw, he was given an urn containing Polish soil which would later be sprinkled on his grave. He would never see his native land again. In Paris, he lived the life of a virtuoso, admired by the local elite. He performed concerts, composed and gave piano lessons. There he met the well-known writer Aurora Dudevant using the pseudonym George Sand, with whom he was romantically involved for several years. Together they travelled to Spanish Majorca to nurse the ailing Fryderyk back to health. Chopin was suffering from tuberculosis, but for quite some time his doctors had dismissed his ailment as a non-threatening sore throat. Unfortunately, the composer's health continued to deteriorate, and he composed and performed less and less. In 1848, he travelled to London and Scotland. In London, he gave his last concert to benefit Polish émigrés. He died in Paris in 1849.

Chopin had already been regarded as a musical genius as both a composer and virtuoso by his contemporaries. His compositions were able to extract from the piano a dynamic, hitherto unencountered potential, producing rich, undreamt of world of sounds. His innovations in the realm of harmony enabled his compositions to speak a completely new and surprisingly rich musical language. The balance and perfection of his works endowed them with a touch of classical styles, whilst their poetry and moodiness rank his music within the romantic convention then in vogue. The romantic trait of his compositions was their folk, and hence national component. As Karol Szymanowski once said, in his Mazurkas and Polonaises Chopin wanted to 'take the eternally beating heart of the race in his hands and re-create it in the form of a perfect, universally comprehensible work of art.'

JÓZEF PIŁSUDSKI (1867–1935)

Independence activist, politician, statesman and first Marshal of Poland. The architect of Poland's independent statehood in 1918, he became Interim Chief of State. He was commander-in-chief of Poland's Armed Forces during the Polish-Soviet War of 1920 and the author of the battle plan pf the Battle of Warsaw, known as 'the Miracle of the Vistula'. Fought on 12-25 August 1920 between Polish forces and the Soviet Army under General Tukha-

chevsky, it has been acknowledged as one of the decisive battles in world history. It enabled Poland to maintain its hard-won independence and stopped the expansion of the communist revolution to Western Europe. Piłsudski had advocated an Inter-Sea Confederation comprising the lands of the former Polish-Lithuanian Commonwealth. But it was his opponent Roman Dmowski's concept of a more compact national state that won out. In view of the political crisis engulfing Poland, Piłsudski decided on a military coup carried out on 12-14 May 1926 with the support of a majroity of Poles.

Józef Piłsudski.

Jan Kiliński.

JAN KILIŃSKI (1760–1819)

A cobbler by trade, during the 1794 Kościuszko Insurrection against Russian occupation he led the townspeople of Warsaw into battle. He was the only representative of the middle burgher class appointed by the king to membership of the Provisional Substitute Council which assumed power in Warsaw during the insurrection. For his service, he was nominated a colonel by Tadeusz Kościuszko. Arrested by the Prussians and handed over to the Russians, Kiliński was exiled into the depths of Russian. Upon his return he wrote memoirs.

MARIA SKŁODOWSKA-CURIE (1867–1934)

Born in Warsaw at Freta Street 16, this outstanding chemist and physicist spent most of her life in France. There she studied and pursued her scientific career. Among her main achievements was her theory of radiation and the discovery of two new elements: Radium and Polonium. She also conducted research on the use of radiation therapy in the treatment of cancer. She was twice awarded the Nobel Prize: in 1903 with her husband Pierre in Physics and in 1911 in Chemistry.

HENRYK SIENKIEWICZ (1846–1916)

A novelist and journalist of the positivist period, he ranked amongst the world's most popular writers, whose works were translated into many different languages including Arabic and Japanese. His favourite literary form was the historical

Maria Skłodowska-Curie.

novel. In Poland, the greatest popularity was enjoyed by his "Trilogy" comprising "With Fire and Sword", "Pan Wołodyjowski" and "The Deluge". His novel "Quo Vadis" gained the greatest popularity abroad. His novels "Knights of the Cross" and 'In Desert and Wilderness' also won a considerable following. In 1905, he was awarded the Nobel Literary Prize for his overall literary achievements. In 1900, Sienkiewicz received a manor house in Oblęgorek near Kielce as a gift from the Polish nation.

ISAAC BASHEVIS SINGER (1904–91)

A well-known writer of Jewish ancestry, he wrote in Yiddish. For quite some time, he had lived at Krochmalna street in Warsaw and had his writings printed in the Warsaw journal "Literarisze Bleter". In 1936, he emigrated to the United States. In 1978, he was awarded the Nobel Prize for Literature. His works include the novel 'The Magician of Lublin'.

JAN KIEPURA (1902–66)

A popular singer (tenor) and actor, he began his artistic career on the stage of the Warsaw Opera and gained his first international exposure in Vienna. He performed at the world's most prestigious venues including La Scala, Covent Garden and the Metropolitan Opera. He was also known as a silver-screen star appearing in numerous films produced by Hollywood and German studios.

IGNACY PADEREWSKI (1860-1941)

An outstanding pianist, composer, politician and independence activist, he studied music at the Warsaw Institute of Music and launched his solo career at the Warsaw Philharmonic. He achieved international renown performing abroad in such countries as France and the United States. He also was involved in diplomatic efforts on behalf of Poland's independence. After Poland and regained its independence, he returned to Poland where in 1919 he became the prime minister and foreign minister.

Ignacy Paderewski.

Old Town

The Barbican, which provided additional fortification to the New Town Gate.

Gunpowder Bastion is a part of the town's preserved defensive walls.

A monument to a Young Freedom-Fighter, sculpted by Jerzy Jarnuszkiewicz, adorns the Old Town walls.

The Augustinian Monastery and Church of St Martin is situated along Piwna Street, one of the picturesque streets of Old Town.

Cobbler Jan Kiliński, a hero of the Kościuszko Insurrection, is portrayed by the 1936 monument of sculptor Stanisław Jackowski which stands in Podwale Street.

The column of King Sigismund III Vasa - the pride of Castle Square - is Warsaw's oldest secular monument.

Stone Steps are one of the most picturesque Old Town pasageways. Originally

Historical Museum of Warsaw.

The Statue of the Mermaid, the symbol of Warsaw, was unveiled in the Old Town Marketplace in 1855.

The church of Our Lady of Grace (No. 10 Świętojańska Street), founded by King Zygmunt III, was erected in 1608-26 in the style of the late Renaissance.

St John's Cathedral, Warsaw's oldest church, was erected round the turn of the 14th century.

The Royal Castle was built for King Zygmunt III Vasa afterPoland's capital had been moved to Warsaw.

The Sheet-Metal-Roofed Palace was built in 1720 for Jerzy Dominik Lubomirski and his wife, Magdalena of Tarło.

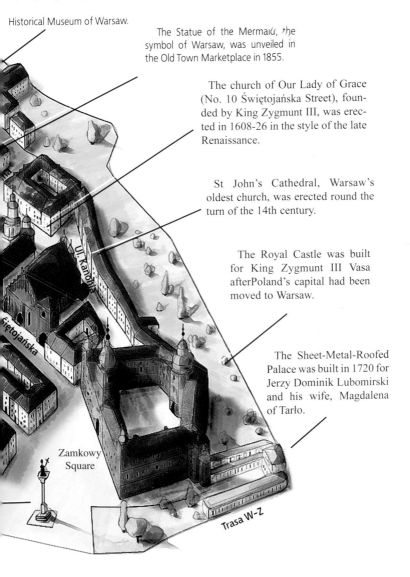

Ul. Kanonie

Świętojańska

Zamkowy Square

Trasa W-Z

1. Old Town marked the start of Warsaw's urban development. The town's incorporation and the bringing-in of settlers round the turn of the 14th century was the work of Duke Bolesław II of Płock. Forty parcels of land were mapped out in a chessboard pattern round the square marketplace. By the end of the 14th century, the town was enclosed by a defensive wall independent of the castle's fortifications. At that time, the entire town occupied an area of 10 hectares and counted several hundred inhabitants. Over the centuries there appeared numerous structures that were to give Old Town its unique flavour. The inclusion of Warsaw's Old Town on UNESCO's World Heritage List attests to that fact.

2. The Royal Castle was built for King Zygmunt III Vasa afterPoland's capital had been moved to Warsaw. The construction of anew residence on a pentagonal plan was entrusted to Italian architects,Giovanni Trevano, Giacomo Rodondo and Matteo Castelli. The castle underwent numerous renovations and expansion schemes in the centuries that followed. Burnt in 1939, its flame-gutted ruins were blown up in 1944. The castle was rebuilt through public donations in 1971-84.

3. The ballroom was created in a wing built on during the reign of King August III. It was fitted and appointed in 1777-81 at the behest of King Stanisław August Poniatowski according to a design by Dominik Merlini, the chief royal architect. In addition to its superb sculpted decorations, the ballroom is crowned by a 150 square metre plafond painted by Marcello Bacciarelli.

4. The interior décor of the Royal Castle's Marble Room was created during the reign of King Wadysław IV, the son of King Zygmunt III. During the castle's major renovation undertaken by King Stanisław August Poniatowski, a portrait gallery of Polish kings, painted by Marcello Bacciarelli, was added.

5. After 1722, during the reign of King August II, the Senate Hall was moved from the ground floor of the Great Court to the first floor, where its windows opened on today's Castle Square. The hall's décor was designed by Saxon architect Joachim Daniel Jauch.

1. The Augustinian Monastery and Church of St Martin is situated along Piwna Street, one of the picturesque streets of Old Town. Founded by Duke Siemowit of Masovia. The monastery was completely remodelled in the late-Baroque style in 1631-36 and at the start of the 18th century. The church's superb 'wavy' façade was designed during the last renovation by Karol Bay.

2. The church of Our Lady of Grace (No. 10 Świętojańska Street), founded by King Zygmunt III, was erected in 1608-26 in the style of the late Renaissance.

3. Kanonia is a small triangular square on the site of a former graveyard. It owes its name to the dwelling-houses along its rim which were once inhabited by canons of the Warsaw chapter.

4-5. St John's Cathedral, Warsaw's oldest church, was erected round the turn of the 14th century. Originally, it fulfilled the role of the local parish church and the castle chapel. In the 14th century, it took on its present form of three Gothic halls of equal size. At present it serves as the archcathedral. In 1837-42, it was completely remodelled and given an English-style Gothic façade.

1. The Statue of the Mermaid, the symbol of Warsaw, was unveiled in the Old Town Marketplace in 1855. Konstanty Hegel drew his inspiration from earlier portrayals of the half-woman/half-fish dating from the 14th century.

2. The double portal of Wilczkowski House (No. 21 Marketplace) dates from 1608, when Warsaw Old Town Mayor Paweł Zembrzuski built his seat there. The 18th-century political reformer Hugo Kołłątaj had lived and died in the house.

3. The Little Negro Boy House was built at the start of the 17th century for Italian merchant Jakub Gianotti. The head of the Negro boy was meant to symbolise the business of the house owner who dealt in overseas goods.

4. Stone Steps are one of the most picturesque Old Town pasageways. Originally, water from the Vistula was carried up the stepsthrough a no longer existing White Gate.

5. The Barbican, which provided additional fortification to the New Town Gate, was built in 1548 by Jan Baptysta of Venice. It was the youngest element of the town's fortifications and originally included a drawbridge. At present, it is a summer arts and crafts gallery.

6. A monument to a Young Freedom-Fighter, sculpted by Jerzy Jarnuszkiewicz, adorns the Old Town walls. It commemorates the children and youths who took part in the 1944 Warsaw Uprising.

7. Gunpowder Bastion is a part of the town's preserved defensive walls. Built from the mid-14th to the mid-16th century, they comprised a double ring of fortified walls, bolstered at intervals by bastions and towers.

1. New Town developed beyond the New Town Gate round the turn of the 15th century along the road to Zakroczym. On the strength of a privilege granted in 1408, it became an independent urban entity. It had its own marketplace, town hall of municipal authorities, but was not surrounded by fortifications. It was joined to Warsaw in 1791. The New Town Marketplace had originally been rectangular in shape and had covered nearly twice the area of the Old Town Marketplace. In the course of successive modernisations the marketplace took on an irregular shape.

2. St Casimir's Church of the Sisters of the Blessed Sacrament was founded by Queen Marysieńka Sobieska. Built in 1688-89, it was an outstanding achievement of architect Tylman of Gameren.

3-4. The Church of the Blessed Virgin Mary is Warsaw's oldest preserved church. Its construction got under way in 1411 at the behest of the Anna Danuta Kiejstut, wife of Masovia's Duke Janusz the Elder and wacompleted in 1492.

5. In 2011 in Podzamcze, by the Vistula, at the height of the Blessed Virgin Mary Church, the largest multimedia fountain in Europe was founded. Through pumps which eject 3000 gallons of water per minute a 3 mm thick wall of water was obtained, 10 m high and 30 m long. Images of the capital, accompanied by sound, are displayed on the water.

6. The Franciscan Church of St Francis Seraphic was built in 1680--1733 according to a design by Jan Chrzciciel Ceroni. In 1788, JózefBo-retti remodelled its façade and elevated its tower.

1. The Rococo Sapieha Palace (No. 6 Zakroczymska Street) was built in 1731-46 by architect Jan Zygmunt Deybel for the chancellor of the Grand Duchy of Lithuania, Jan Fryderyk Sapieha. Re-modelled in the 19th century, it served as military barracks.

2. The building in which Maria Skłodowska-Curie was born in 1867 and live until she was 24 at No. 16 Freta Street now houses a museum in her honour. It contains mementoes linked to the Nobel Prize laureate, including photographs, documents and medals.

3. The Dominican Church of St Hyacinth was built in 1612-38 according to the partially Gothic-influenced design of Italian architect Jan Włoch.

4. The Pauline Church of the Holy Ghost was built in 1699-1717 according to a design by Józef Piolo and Józef Szymon Bellotti. King Jan Kazimierz granted the site to the Pauline Fathers after the Swedish "deluge" (invasion).

5. The Church of Our Lady Queen of the Polish Crown (Krasiński Square) was built in 1660-82 by Tytus Buratini and in 1758-69 was given a new Palladian façade by Jakub Fontana. At present the church is the Field Cathedral of the Polish Armed Forces and the seat of their Chaplain General.

6. The Monument to the 1944 Warsaw Uprising, created by sculptor Wincenty Kućma and architect Jacek Budyn, was unveiled in Krasiński Square in 1989. It portrays freedom-fighters defending a barricade and descending into the sewers, one of whose openings is near the statue.

1. The classicist building of the Wielki Theatre was built in 1825-33 according to a design by Antoni Corazzi, assisted by Ludwik Kozubowski. It boasts Europe's biggest opera stage, can accommodate an audience of 1,900.

2. The building of the Society for the Encouragement of the Fine Arts (Zachęta) was built according to a design by Stefan Szyller in the academic Renaissance style in 1898-1903. The society was established by Polish painters to popularise contemporary Polish art. The purchase of outstanding art works, moved in 1940 to the National Museum, was organised. Today the building contains an art gallery.

3. The classicist Augsburg Evangelical (Lutheran) Church of the Holy Trinity was built in 1777-81 according to a design by Bogumi Zug.

4. The site of today's Palace of culture and Science before World War Two had been an area of densely built-up tenements lining Zielna, Śliska, Sienna, Chmielna and Złota streets. Traces of those streets may be seen on the commemorative plaques set into the pavement along the paths surrounding the Placa of Culture.

5. Built in 1901-11 according to a design of Józef Pius Dziekoński, the Church of the Redeemer reflects architectural elements of the Polish Renaissance and Baroque.

6. Constitution Square was part of the city's socialist realistic development planned during the times of President Bolesław Bierut.

7. The building of the Warsaw Polytechnic was built in 1899-1901, chiefly by architect Stefan Szyller. Inside is a magnificent four-storey hall fringed with galleries and topped with a skylight.

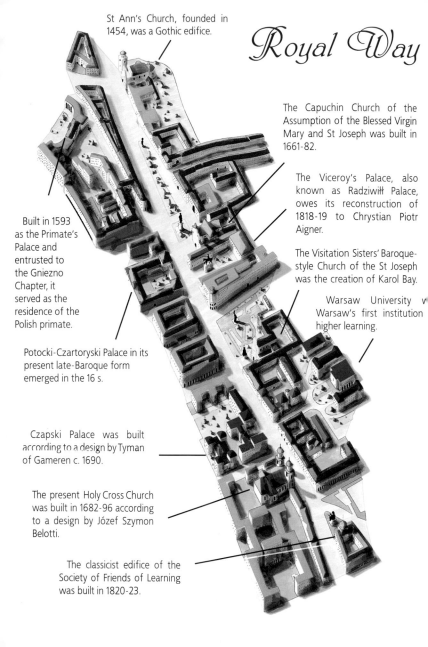

Royal Way

St Ann's Church, founded in 1454, was a Gothic edifice.

The Capuchin Church of the Assumption of the Blessed Virgin Mary and St Joseph was built in 1661-82.

The Viceroy's Palace, also known as Radziwiłł Palace, owes its reconstruction of 1818-19 to Chrystian Piotr Aigner.

The Visitation Sisters' Baroque-style Church of the St Joseph was the creation of Karol Bay.

Warsaw University was Warsaw's first institution of higher learning.

Built in 1593 as the Primate's Palace and entrusted to the Gniezno Chapter, it served as the residence of the Polish primate.

Potocki-Czartoryski Palace in its present late-Baroque form emerged in the 16 s.

Czapski Palace was built according to a design by Tyman of Gameren c. 1690.

The present Holy Cross Church was built in 1682-96 according to a design by Józef Szymon Belotti.

The classicist edifice of the Society of Friends of Learning was built in 1820-23.

1. The Royal Way was a route created in the 17th century that led from the Royal Castle (Krakowskie Przedmieście Street, photo 143) to the summer palace of King Stanisław August Poniatowski in Łazienki Park. It was along that route, leading via Czersk to Kraków, that Old Warsaw first developed.

2. Mariensztat, situated behind St Ann's Church at the foot of the escarpment, developed on the site of a jurisdiction (private town) belonging to Maria Potocka. An open-air market existed there from 1847 to 1944. After the war, it was rebuilt in a totally new form, when what was then the modern East-West Thoroughfare was being constructed.

3-4. The Baroque interior of St Ann's Church features illusion-producing frescoes, painted by Bernardine monk Walenty Żebrowski, as well as rococo altars. Worthy of note are the chapels to Blessed Ładysław of Gielniów and Our Lady of Loretto.

1. The Viceroy's Palace, also known as Radziwiłł Palace, owes its reconstruction of 1818-19 to Chrystian Piotr Aigner. Today it is the residence of Poland's president. In front of the palace stands a monument to Prince Józef Poniatowski sculpted by Bertel Thorvaldsen.

2. The Capuchin Church of the Assumption of the Blessed Virgin Mary and St Joseph was built in 1661-82. Its 1782 façade, the work of Efraim Schroeger, was one of the

3. Potocki-Czartoryski Palace in its present late-Baroque form emerged in the 1660 s. Szymon Bogumił Zug and Jan Christian Kamsetzer designed its interior for Princess Izabela Lubomirska. Two decorative grates, executed according to the 1896 drawings of Leonard Marconi, grace the palace entrance.

4. Warsaw University was Warsaw's first institution of higher learning. It was established in 1816 at the initiative of such people as Stanisław Staszic. Kazimierz Palace, now the seat of the university's rector and senate, was built for King Władysław IV and later renovated for King Jan Kazimierz.

5. The Visitation Sisters' Baroque-style Church of the St Joseph was the creation of Karol Bay in 1728-33. Its unusual façade and interior were designed somewhat later by Efraim Schroeger. The main altar came from the workshop of Jan Jerzy Plersz. Many valuable paintings have been preserved in the church including Tadeusz Kuntze-Konicz's Visitaiton in the main altar and Daniel Szulc's St Louis Gonzaga.

6. The present Holy Cross Church was built in 1682-96 according to a design by Józef Szymon Belotti. In 1726-54, the Brothers Fontana erected a façade adorned with the figures of the Apostles Peter and Paul, the work of sculptor Jan Jerzy Plersz. Inside, affixed to a pillar is a plaque commemorating Fryderyk Chopin and beneath it - an urn containing his heart. The church contains the heart of Frederic Chopin.

1. The classicist edifice of the Society of Friends of Learning was built in 1820-23 according to Antonio Corazzi's design and is known as Staszic Palace after the name of its founder. The Nicholas Copernicus monument was set erected in 1830 in front of Staszic Palace at the initiative of Stanisław Staszic. The author of the monument was Bertel Thorvaldsen.

3. Ostrogski Castle is the seat of the Fryderyk Chopin Society which gathers mementoes and documents relating to Poland's world-renow-ned composer. The late-16th-century palace, which underwent-numerous renovations including that carried out by Józef Fontana in 1752, acquired its present appearance in the 19th century.

4. Nowy Świat Street is an important stretch of the Royal Way. Not built up until the end of the 18th century, it boasts many interesting dwelling-houses and palaces.

5. At the centre of Three Crosses Square stands ther Classicist Church of St Alexander, designed by Chrystian Piotr Aigner and built in 1818-26. The cupolated rotunda alludes to the Pantheon of Rome.

6. The Home Army Memorial is dedicated to the soldiers and civilian collaborators of the Polish underground of 1939-1945.

7. The Polish Sejm (parliament) Building was erected in 1925-28 according to the design of Kazimierz Skurewicz. The semi-rotunda housing its main assembly hall dates from that period.

8. Ujazdów Castle, perched on the Vistula escarpment, was built on orders from King Zygmunt III Vasa in 1624. It was later remodelled by such famous architects as Tylman of Gameren, Dominik Merlini and Stanisław Zawadzki. Burnt and dismantled down to its foundation, it re-emerged anew in 1973 to serve as a Centre of Contemporary Art.

9. Belvedere Palace owes its name to the beautiful view (belle vedere) that can be enjoyed from its garden. Its classicist form was created in 1819-22 by Jakub Kubicki for the tsarist viceroy, Prince Constantine. Between the two World Wars and also at the start of the Third Republic is was the seat of Poland's presidents. Józef Piłsudski, Poland's great pre-war leader, also resided there. His monument has been erected next to the palace.

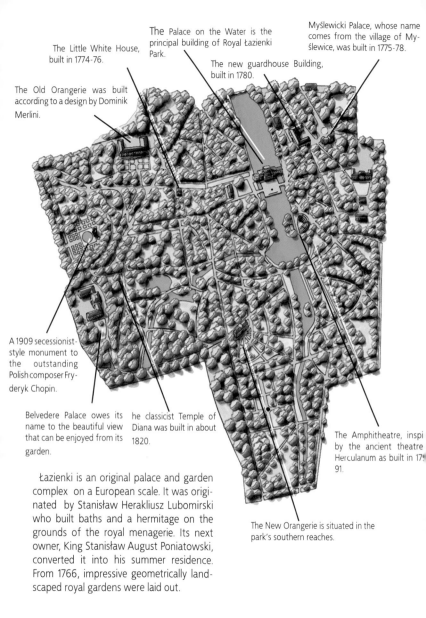

The Little White House, built in 1774-76.

The Palace on the Water is the principal building of Royal Łazienki Park.

Myślewicki Palace, whose name comes from the village of Myślewice, was built in 1775-78.

The new guardhouse Building, built in 1780.

The Old Orangerie was built according to a design by Dominik Merlini.

A 1909 secessionist-style monument to the outstanding Polish composer Fryderyk Chopin.

Belvedere Palace owes its name to the beautiful view that can be enjoyed from its garden.

he classicist Temple of Diana was built in about 1820.

The Amphitheatre, inspi by the ancient theatre Herculanum as built in 17 91.

Łazienki is an original palace and garden complex on a European scale. It was originated by Stanisław Herakliusz Lubomirski who built baths and a hermitage on the grounds of the royal menagerie. Its next owner, King Stanisław August Poniatowski, converted it into his summer residence. From 1766, impressive geometrically landscaped royal gardens were laid out.

The New Orangerie is situated in the park's southern reaches.

Łazienki

1-2. The Palace on the Water is the principal building of Royal Łazienki Park. The original baths, designed by Tylman of Gameren, were built by Stanisław Herakliusz Lubomirski in about 1680. During the reign of King Stanisław August Poniatowski, a classicist palace designed by Dominik Merlini arose. Its northern façade was given a columned portico.

3. The classicist Ballroom was added to the palace in 1788. Its décor was the work of Jan Chrystian Kamsetzer.

4. Salomon's Hall is an elegant room reminiscent of a biblical temple. Its walls were adorned with the paintings of Marcello Bacciarelli.

1-2. The Little White House, built in 1774-76, was the first structure erected by Stanisław August in the Łazienki grounds. The wooden building, most likely the work of Dominik Merlini, reflects a villa style of architecture. Rich decorative painting adorns its interior. An example is the Dining Room, completely covered with paintings of the grotesque variety created by Jan Bogumił Plersz, which became a model for many later classicist residences.

3. The Old Orangerie was built according to a design by Dominik Merlini. It houses a theatre, one of the world's few surviving examples of an 18th-century court theatre.

4. The New Orangerie is situated in the park's southern reaches. It was built in 1860 according to a design developed by Adam Adolf Loeve and Józef Orłowski. In keeping with its original purpose, it houses various exotic plants.

5. The classicist Temple of Diana was built in about 1820 to resemble an ancient Greek temple.

6. The Amphitheatre, inspired by the ancient theatre in Herculanum, was built in 1790-91 according to a design conceived by Jan Chrystian Kamsetzer. The stage on the little island, on which performances take place to this day, was provided with column ruins reminiscent of Jove's Temple in Baalbeck.

7-8. Myślewicki Palace, whose name comes from the village of Myślewice, was built in 1775-78 according to a design developed by Dominik Merlini. To its sides were added quarter-circular wings ending in pavilions, and thus a palace with classicist features came into being. It survived the Second World War and boasts a splendid interior. Views of Rome and Venice painted by Jan Bogumił Plersz have been preserved in the Dining Room pictured here.

9. A 1909 secessionist-style monument to the outstanding Polish composer Fryderyk Chopin was unveiled in Łazienki Park in 1926. In summer, Sunday piano recitals are held at the foot of the monument. In 1940 the statue was blown up by Germans and taken to mills.

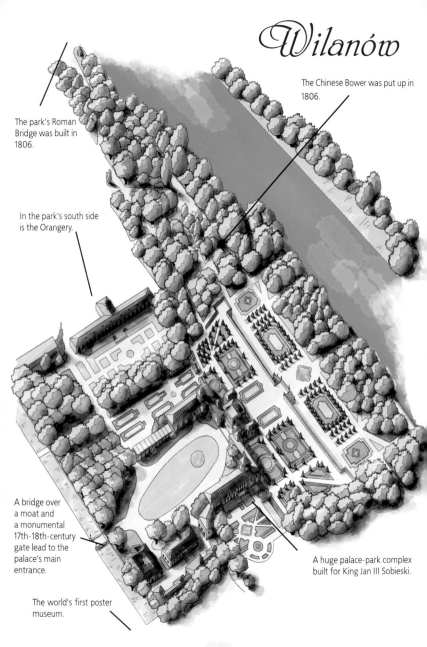

Wilanów

The Chinese Bower was put up in 1806.

The park's Roman Bridge was built in 1806.

In the park's south side is the Orangery.

A bridge over a moat and a monumental 17th-18th-century gate lead to the palace's main entrance.

The world's first poster museum.

A huge palace-park complex built for King Jan III Sobieski.

~~~~~~~ Wilanów ~~~~~~~

1. St Ann's Church owes its neo-Renaissance appearance to the renovation carried out in 1857-70 under the supervision of Henryk andLeander Marconi and Jan Huss.

2-3. The Mausoleum of Stanisław Kostka and Aleksandra Potocki was built in 1836 by their son Aleksander. The neo-Gothic work of Henryk Marconi is adorned with sculptures by Jakub Tatarkiewicz and Konstanty Hegel.

4. Manège and Coach-house designed by Franciszek Maria Lanci and built in 1848 roku. After the Second World War, only the building's façade survived. A modern pavilion was built onto it, and in 1963 the world's first poster museum was opened there.

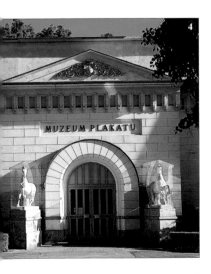

1-2. In this southern district of Warsaw is found a huge palace-park complex built for King Jan III Sobieski. The original none-too-big manor house called Villa Nova, was transformed into a Baroque-style palatial residence. The oldest part of Wilanów Palace is its main hull. It was built according to a design by Augustyn Locci in 1681-96 for Jan III Sobieski. In 1732-29, wings on both sides of its forecourt were added. Work on the palace continued with interruptions until the end of the 19th century.

3. A supraporta in the form of a lion's skin symbolises the courage and bravery of King John III Sobieski. It was placed above the doorway of the garden-side wall.

4. The Baroque décor of the King's Bed Chamber is accentuated by a posted bed whose canopy was sewn from Turkish fabric captured by King Jan III Sobieski at the Battle of Vienna.

5.. The King's Ante-Chamber is adorned with rich stuccowork and painted decorations. The ceiling is contains a plafond depicting Winter, painted by Jerzy Eleuter Siemiginowski, and the stuccowork was executed by Andrzej Schlüter.

3. When the palace was being built, a twin level Baroque-style garden was created - the work of Italian Adolfo Boy. The patchwork of lawns and box-shrub-lined lanes was laid out in keeping with the geometric principles of the times.

4. The Chinese Bower was put up in 1806.

1. The destruction of World War Two particularly affected the area round today's Palace of Culture and Science. From the 1980s, office towers dominating the city-centre skyline began arising on the site of the war-ravaged pre-war urban tenements.

2. Hotel Marriott (Aleje Jerozolimskie 65/79), which is 170 metres tall, was built in the 1980s. Apart from the hotel, the building's 20 top storeys contain the offices of Polish LOT Airline. Next to it stands the 150-metre-tall Intraco II office tower, built in 1979.

3. In the direct proximity of the Central Railway station is the Złote Tarasy (Golden Terraces) office-shopping-recereational centre. It got its name from Złota Street, where the building was constructed in 2002--07. The generally accessible atrium at its centre is topped by a 10,000 metre^2 undulating roof comprising 4,780 glass triangles with up to 3-metre-long sides.

4. The Metropolitan office building (at Piłsudski Square) was designed by world-renowned architect Sir Norman Foster and built in 2003.

5. The building of Warsaw University Library (Dobra Street 55/66), completed in 1999, roku, was the work of Marek Budzyński and Zbigniew Badowski. It contains nearly three million volumes.

6. The Supreme Court and Appeals Court building was built at Krasiński Square in 1999. It is adorned by "Columns of Law" displaying quotations from Roman law. On the Nowiniarska Street side, three sculptures symbolising Faith, Hope and Charity are reflected by a pool.

1. Modern Polish Television building at Samochodowa Street in Mokotów district.

2. The Olympic Centre (Wybrzeże Gdyńskie 4) was built in Żoliborz district in 2003-04 on a plateau overlooking the Vistula. The modern building was designed by Bogdan Kulczyński and Paweł Pyłek. In front of tis entrance stands a sculpture of Icarus, the work of Igor Mitoraj.

3. The Blue Tower was built in 1991 at Bank Square at the former site of the Great Synagogue at Tłomackie Street, destroyed in the last war. Jewish organisations agreed to the skyscraper's construction on condition that it included a hall of Jewish memory.

4. The 10th-Anniversary Stadium on the Vistula in Praga's Kamionek quarter was built in 1954-55 as an Olympic stadium accommodating 71,000 spectators. Its rim was built upon the rubble of the city which had been destroyed during the Warsaw Uprising and in the early post-war years. At present, a National Stadium is being built on the site of the 10th-Anniversary Stadium. At the 10th-Anniversary Stadium site, due to hold the European Football Championships UEFA Euro in 2012, a modern National Stadium was built. It can accommodate 58,500 spectators.

1. Nieborów Palace was built for the Archbishop of Gniezno, Michał Stanisław Radziejowski, in 1690-96 according to Tylman of Gameren's design. French-style gardens were laid out round the palace.

2. A romantic park was laid out in Arcadia, not far from Nieborów, in 1778 for Duchess Helena Przeździecka-Radziwiłł. It contains many structures typical of that type of park, including Gothic castle ruins, Sibyl's Temple, the Arched House of the Margrave and an aqueduct.

3. In Łowicz, west of Warsaw, villagers don their colourful folk attire to take part in processions held on Corpus Christi.

4. The ruins of Czersk Castle are all that remains of the former capital of the Duchy of Masovia before it was moved to Warsaw in 1413. The castle arose at the start of the 15th century on the ruins of an earlier structure. Three round towers have survived. A draw-bridge leads to the castle.

5. Konstancin-Jeziorna is a spa siturated south of Warsaw and popular with Warsaw residents since the late 19th century. The many splendid villas built there in the early 20th century were designed by the greatest architects of the day and reflected a variety of styles.

6. The palace in Otwock Wielki was built in the late 1680s for Kazimierz Ludwik Bieliński. During the times of Grand Crown Marshal Franciszek Bieliński, after whom Warsaw's Marszałkowska Street was named, two side towers designed by royal architect Jakub Fontana were added on in 1757.

1. Classicist Jabłonna Palace was built in 1774-78 for Michał Jerzy Poniatowski according to a design conceived by Dominik Merlini. Its interior was conceived by Szymon Bogumił Zug.

2. The Baroque church in Kobyłka from 1741-45 boast magnificent wall paintings.

3. Liw Castle was built in the late 14th century and served as the seat of the dukes of Masovia. At present, it houses a collection of old weapons and a gallery of portraits from the 18th and 19th centuries.

4. The Milusin manor house in Sulejówek was built in 1923 by thePo-lish Soldier's Committee for Józef Piłsudski. It went up on a parcel of land belonging to his wife Aleksandra née Szczerbińska. In 1923-26, Marshal Piłsudski withdrew from public life to his manor house where he systematically stayed in later years as well.

5. The Gothic castle in Pułtusk was built for the bishops of Płock in the 15th century on the ashes of a 12th-century fortress that had been destroyed in a blaze. During the Renaissance a Great Hall was added, and during the Baroque period two characteristic towers were built onto the entrance gate. At present the structure is the seat of Polonia House.

6. The Gothic-Renaissance Basilica of the Annunciation of the BVM and St Matthew in Pułtusk was built in 1439-49 and in the 1540s. Its main nave together with the presbytery is covered with cradle vaulting.

7. The Gothic castle of the Dukes of Masovia on the River Łyna was built in Ciechanów most likely in 1427-29 by a builder named Niklos. Subsequently elevated on two separate occasions, it was destroyed by the Swedes in 1657. In disuse from the latter half of the 18th century, it is now open to visitors as a regional museum.

TOURIST INFORMATION

Police Station
phone: 22 997
FIRE SERVICE
phone: 22 998
MEDICAL EMERGENCY
phone: 22 999
The Municipal of Warsaw
phone: 22 598 68 00
Number Information in English
phone: 118 811
The International Numbers Office
phone: 118 912
Orders Agency, phone: 19 497
Lost & Found Office.
phone: 22 443 29 60
Lost & Found in Public Transport
phone: 22 663 32 97
TOURIST INFORMATION OFFICES
16 Rozbrat St., phone: 22 194 31

TRANSPORT
LOT INFORMATION
phone: 801 703 703
Bus Information
phone: 703 403 330

Train Information
phone: 22 194 36
URBAN TRANSPORT INFORMATION
phone: 22 194 84

MUSEUMS:
The National Museum
3 Aleje Jerozolimskie, phone: 22 621 10 31
Fryderyk Chopin Museum
Tamka St., phone: 22 441 62 74
Warsaw Uprising Museum
79 Grzybowska St., phone: 22 539 79 06
Zacheta National Art Gallery
3 Stanislaw Malachowski Square,
phone: 22 556 96 00
Centre for Contemporary Art Ujazdowski Castle
2 Jazdów St., phone: 22 628 12 71
The Great Theatre
1 Theatre Square, phone: 22 826 04 23

Page 1: The Royal Castle.
The photographs in this album are from the Jabłoński Family Archives.
Telephone: +48 (22) 642-06-71; cellphone: +48 602 324 409;
website: www.fotojablonski.pl,
e-mail:archiwum@fotojablonski.pl
Graphic design by Paweł and Rafał Jabłoński
ISBN 978-83-61511-69-4

FESTINA Publishers Warsaw
tel/fax +48 (22) 842-54-53, cellphone: +48 602 324 409
e-mail: wydawnictwo@festina.org.pl
www.festina.org.pl

WARSAW